A Kid's Guide to
Martial Arts

D0001487

JUJITSU

Alix Wood

PowerKiDS
press

New York

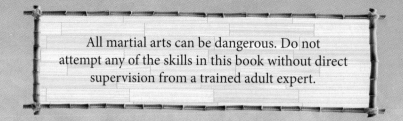

All martial arts can be dangerous. Do not attempt any of the skills in this book without direct supervision from a trained adult expert.

Published in 2013 by The Rosen Publishing Group, Inc.
29 East 21st Street, New York, NY 10010

Copyright © 2013 Alix Wood Books

Editor: Sara Antill
Designer: Alix Wood
Consultant: Sandra Beale-Ellis, National Association of Karate and Martial Art Schools (NAKMAS)

With grateful thanks to Finnian Cooling and everyone at Kernow Martial Arts; James, Joshua, and Elaine Latus, Olivia and Dereka Antonio, Solomon Brown, Ryan Fletcher, Alex Gobbitt, Hayden Hambly, Max Keeling, Joshua Nowell, Kyanna and Katie-Marie Orchard, Natasha Shear, Niamh Stephen, Chris Tanner, Jazmine Watkins, and Emily.

Photo Credits: Cover, 1, 4, 5, 6, 7 top, 8, 9, 11 top and bottom, 19 bottom, 28, 29, 30 © Shutterstock; p7 bottom Yoshitoshi Tsukioka, all other images © Chris Robbins

Library of Congress Cataloging-in-Publication Data

Wood, Alix.
Jujitsu / by Alix Wood.
    p. cm. — (A kid's guide to martial arts)
Includes index.
 ISBN 978-1-4777-0317-5 (library binding) — ISBN 978-1-4777-0356-4 (pbk.) —
ISBN 978-1-4777-0357-1 (6-pack)
1. Jiu-jitsu—Juvenile literature. I. Title.
 GV1114.W654 2013
 796.815'2—dc23

                    2012026856

Manufactured in the United States of America

CPSIA Compliance Information: Batch #WI3PK2: For Further Information contact: Rosen Publishing, New York, New York at 1-800-237-9932

Contents

What Is Jujitsu?

Jujitsu is a martial art from Japan. It was developed as a way of defeating an armed and armored opponent using no weapon, or only a short weapon.

JAPAN

Mimasaka • Tokyo

Map of Japan

Jujitsu was invented by Hisamori Takeuchi, a military man from Mimasaka province, in Japan. Hisamori developed jujitsu from various Japanese martial arts. It was used on the battlefield in close **combat** situations, where weapons were not very useful. Chinese and Korean martial arts mainly used strikes. Japanese hand-to-hand combat, though, used throws, locks, and chokes. Striking techniques weren't any good if your opponent was wearing armor. Later, some striking was introduced to jujitsu, mainly as a way to distract opponents or to unbalance them before using another technique.

FLEXIBILITY IS STRENGTH

A doctor, Akiyama Yoshitoki, founded the *Yoshin Ryu* style of jujitsu. While at a mountain retreat developing his jujitsu skills, Akiyama watched the willow trees bend under the weight of the snow. Their branches didn't break like other trees, because they were **flexible**. He realized that bending can stop you from breaking.

Jujitsu means the "gentle art." It relies on technique rather than strength. Jujitsu uses the force of the attacker and turns it against him. Jujitsu encourages awareness, confidence, and **adaptability**, all useful skills for self-defense. Today jujitsu is practiced in both traditional and modern sport forms. The Olympic sport and martial art of judo came from jujitsu. Brazilian jiu-jitsu comes from early Kodokan judo and is a very popular martial art. This book will mainly look at traditional jujitsu.

The Samurai

*Jujitsu was the martial art used by medieval warriors of Japan called the **samurai**. The samurai came from noble families and were fierce fighters. Each family developed their own style of fighting.*

The samurai swore loyalty to their lord by signing a **contract** using the warrior's blood. Then the contract would be burned, and the ashes were mixed with water for the samurai to drink. The warrior was loyal to his lord, and to die protecting him was his greatest honor. If his lord was killed, the samurai would kill himself to follow the lord into death.

A statue of a samurai warrior

Fighting in Armor

A samurai without weapons could still defend himself. His armor was specially made so he could move but still be protected. Instead of being made of solid sheets of metal, it was jointed and flexible, perfect for jujitsu. The samurai could use his flexibility to throw his opponent. A samurai would often wear a mask to scare his opponents and protect his face. It was useful to hide his own fear, too.

A samurai warrior's armor

As well as being warriors, the samurai were known for their appreciation of writing and the fine arts. They followed a strict code of conduct, called *bushido* in every aspect of life. They were expected to be good at the arts, including poetry, handwriting, and flower arranging.

A samurai prepares to kill himself after losing a battle for his master. He has written his death poem, seen in the top right corner.

Jujitsu Equipment

*When doing jujitsu, you wear a **judogi**. This is a thin, white cotton jacket and pants with a belt tied around the waist.*

Put on the pants on first. Some have a drawstring around the waist. Pull the string tight and then tie it through the loop at the front of the pants.

The jacket is tied by string at either side. The left side goes on top.

The belt is tied over the jacket at the waist. Girls ususally wear a white short sleeve T-shirt under the jacket. Boys do not wear the T-shirt.

It is important to keep your judogi clean.

THE BELT COLORS

Traditional jujitsu belt ranking usually follows this order, but it will vary from school to school.

White — 7th kyu
Yellow — 6th kyu
Orange — 5th kyu
Green — 4th kyu
Blue — 3rd kyu
Purple — 2nd kyu
Brown — 1st kyu
Black — 1st–5th dan

The belt colors show which students have trained longer and have more skill compared to other students. Belt ranking is a new concept. Early martial artists started with a white belt which they never washed. That's why the belt colors tend to get darker as you progress!

How to tie the belt

1 Place the middle of the belt on your stomach.

2 Pass each end of the belt behind you and back to the front.

3 Hold the belt together. Cross the right end over the left end, then thread it up behind both loops.

4 Cross the left end over the right end. Thread the left end back through the hole to finish the knot.

5 Both ends of the belt should be the same length and the ends should fall about halfway between your waist and knees.

The Dojo

The place where you learn jujitsu is called a **dojo**. The dojo can be a multipurpose hall or a specially-built martial arts school. Dojos will usually have some rules and **etiquette** you must learn, like bowing.

The instructor in the class is called the *sensei*, which means "one who has gone before." During class, you should call the instructor "sensei, sir," or "sensei, ma'am." Call other students who are teaching you sir or ma'am, too. This shows respect and thanks them for taking the time to teach you.

This sensei is sitting in a position called seiza. It is a safe and respectful way to sit on the mat. If someone fell on you while practicing, they would be unlikely to hurt you or themselves.

Safety is Important

There are some simple things you can do to make sure you and everyone else stays safe at your dojo.

- Remove all jewelry and watches.
- Tie back long hair.
- Keep your toenails and your fingernails short.

What should this girl do before she enters the dojo?

The bow, or *rei*, is the jujitsu salute. There are two bows, a standing bow and a kneeling bow. For a standing bow, stand with your feet together and your hands on your thighs. Looking at your partner, bend forward for about one second, then stand straight again. This bow is used when entering or leaving the mat and the dojo. It lets others know that you are coming on the mat to practice. It shows respect, and shows you are leaving the worries of life behind you during class.

This boy is doing a kneeling bow from seiza. At the beginning and end of class students bow like this to the sensei and the sensei will return the bow.

11

Warming Up

It is important to warm up before you start your jujitsu session. This will stop you from pulling muscles. Here are some good exercises you can use for your warm-up.

Remember, if you feel any pain, stop what you are doing and move onto a different exercise or stretch. Don't strain anything.

Arm circles

Stand with your feet shoulder width apart.

1 Bring both arms up over your head.

2 Circle your arms down and behind you.

3 Bring your arms back up to the starting position.

Toe grabs

Sit down with both feet straight out in front of you. Reach out and grab your toes and lift up both your feet. Hold and count to three.

Touch the floor

1 Stand with your feet wide apart.

2 Bend down and touch the floor.

3 If you can do this easily, try moving your feet closer together.

13

Jujitsu Basics

*Now you are ready to learn some basics. It is important to learn the basic fighting **stance**. From this stance you can defend yourself, attack, or escape from danger.*

For a fighting stance, stand with your feet shoulder width apart. Raise your hands roughly level with your head and slightly out in front of you so you can block punches and kicks to the head.

Keep your stronger hand back, so if you are right handed, have your right hand back and your left foot forward. Keep your chin down and your eyes looking straight ahead.

Stand about 1.5 feet (0.5 m) away from your opponent. If your opponent moves toward you, take a step back with your back foot and then slide your front foot back to follow it. Do the opposite and move forward toward your opponent if he goes backward.

How to escape from a front strangle

1

This technique is used when your attacker strangles you from the front with her arms straight.

2

Step back with your right foot. This will make your upper body twist and will loosen the strangle slightly.

3

Raise your left hand straight up into the air. Using your left hand, punch through your attacker's arms to break the strangle.

Breakfalls

Breakfalls are very important as they allow you to land from throws as comfortably as possible. You need to learn to fall safely and get back up to protect yourself as quickly as possible.

Side breakfall

Stand with your feet level. Place your right foot in front and to the left of your left foot. Rest the side of your foot on the floor.

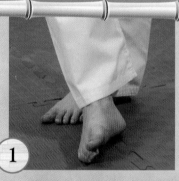

Let yourself fall to the right. As you land, throw your right arm on the floor. This breaks your fall as it takes most of the force.

Bring your left knee up to protect you from possible kicks. Also bring your hands up to your face to protect yourself.

Forward roll

Use a mat to practice your forward roll. This roll can be a breakfall or an escape.

With your right foot in front of your left, drop your right arm toward your left leg and tuck your chin into your chest.

Roll forward along your right arm and shoulder.

Come up on your right foot and twist into your ready stance. Face the direction you just came from.

Back breakfall

From the standing position crouch down and cross your arms over your chest. Be sure to also tuck your chin into your chest.

Now fall onto your back throwing your arms out to the side to break the fall. If an attacker was in front of you, you may want to strike by thrusting your legs to the front.

Strikes

Jujitsu doesn't focus on striking opponents like some other martial arts do. Strikes in jujitsu are usually used as distractions. They help to weaken the opponent so that a hold or lock can be applied.

Forefist punch

Start from the fighting stance, keeping your guard up at all times.

The first strike is using your left fist. This is just a small jab preparing for the next strike.

As you bring your left fist back, strike with your right. Twist your hips and twist on the ball of your rear foot for extra speed and power.

1

Raise your right hand behind your ear, with your left hand slightly forward.

2

Snap your arm and strike while pulling your right arm tight to your waist.

3

Bring your right hand around in front of you.

A hammerfist is a strike with the bottom of a clenched fist. This strike will not damage the bones of the hands. The hammerfist is particularly effective for striking the the wrist when blocking punches.

THE TAP

In jujitsu the usual way to show **submission** is to tap the mat, yourself, or your partner, at least twice, in rapid succession. It is easier and faster than speaking, as well as being safer. If you can't tap with your hands, you may tap with your feet or say "*mate*" which means "stop."

Blocks

The purpose of blocking techniques is to stop the opponent's punch, kick, strike, or grab from succeeding. There are several different types of block.

High block

If your attacker throws a left punch, block it with your left arm. Also twist clockwise on the ball of your left foot.

If your attacker throws a right punch, block it with your right arm. Also twist **counterclockwise** on the ball of your right foot.

Low block

If your attacker kicks with her right foot, you should block it with your right arm.

If your attacker kicks with her left foot, you should block it with your left arm.

Basic inside forearm block

This block is used when your attacker throws a straight punch. Use your left **forearm** to block the strike. At the same time bring your right hand down to your hip.

Kicks

Although jujitsu is best known for its locks, sweeps, and throws, it is a complete battlefield art. Jujitsu training also includes kicks. Jujitsu kicks aren't fancy or acrobatic. They are short strikes meant to either disable an attacker or make him easier to throw to the ground.

Front snap kick

Start from the fighting stance.

Bring your rear leg's knee up to hip height.

Snap your foot out to land the strike. Return to fighting stance in the same way.

Side snap kick

1 Start by standing in fighting stance.

2 Bring your right knee up and twist counterclockwise on the ball of your left foot.

3 You should be facing sideways from your attacker. Now strike your attacker's knee or groin.

4 The strike will probably make your attacker move her front leg back. Return to your position before the strike.

PRACTICE

Try practicing your kicks with a partner. Stop just short of the target. Try training in front of a mirror, too, to get your technique right.

Armlocks

Armlocks are popular for beginners as they are a good way to stop an attack and hold your opponent.

Straight armlock

1 Block the punch with a left-handed downward block.

2 Grab your attacker's wrist with your right hand. Twist on your feet so you are at her side.

3 Strike with your left elbow to the side of your attacker's head.

4 Put your left hand around your attacker's right arm. Grab hold of your judogi and twist her wrist clockwise. Push her hand down to apply the lock.

Shoulder lock

1 As your attacker throws the punch, step forward on your left foot and block with a left-handed downward block.

2 Strike hard with your right palm on to your attacker's right shoulder. This move is called a palm strike.

3 Pull her right shoulder down, with your left hand under her right arm. Twist on your left foot so you are facing sideways.

4 Now put your left hand on top of your right hand. Your attacker's arm should be resting on your left shoulder.

GENTLY

When training, it is important not to apply full pressure when you do an armlock. When you are young your **ligaments** are not fully developed. You can damage a ligament forever if an armlock is done too roughly.

Throws and Holds

Holds are ways of pinning your attacker to the floor. Throws are a good way of getting him there!

Scarf hold

Sit next to your attacker with your back against her side.

Put your right arm around her neck. Grab hold of your judogi or hers to stop her from pulling her neck out.

Take her right arm under your left armpit and pin it there. Grab hold of the back of her right arm.

Tuck your head in and spread your legs as far as possible. This makes it difficult for your attacker to move.

Body drop

When your attacker throws a punch, block the strike with an inside forearm block and step with your left foot to the left of your attacker's left foot.

Now twist counterclockwise on the ball of your left foot. Take your right arm behind your attacker and hold his right arm with your left hand.

Place your right foot to the right of his right foot. Move your left foot further left and bend your left knee. Keep your right leg quite straight with the ball of your foot on the floor.

Twist your upper body counterclockwise with the heel of your right foot on the floor. Your attacker's right leg will be swept back as your right hand drags him over your right leg. Do an armlock, with your left hand around his right arm just behind the elbow.

Learn Japanese

A lot of jujitsu words are in Japanese. The Japanese language uses different symbols to write words. It's fun to learn to recognize some of the symbols.

Japanese has three alphabets! The most commonly used alphabet is **kanji**. Words are made up of picture symbols rather than sounds. Around 50,000 kanji exist, but only about two thousand are used regularly. The other two alphabets are more like English, with 48 symbols that you need to learn for each. The *katakana* alphabet is used for foreign words and names, and the *hiragana* alphabet is used for words there are no kanji for, or sometimes as a translation of the kanji to make it easier for people who don't know kanji well. It can be confusing!

This is the kanji for jujitsu. The top symbol means "gentle" and the bottom symbol means "art."

"Tori" and "uke" are two Japanese words you may hear. "Tori" means someone giving a technique and "uke" means someone receiving a technique. If your partner attacks you, but you block the attack and throw your partner, you are "tori." So, the words "tori" and "uke" don't just mean attacker and defender. The role is decided by who completes a successful technique, not by who starts the attack.

Counting in Japanese

English	Japanese	Symbol
one	ichi	一
two	ni	二
three	san	三
four	shi	四
five	go	五
six	roku	六
seven	shichi	七
eight	hachi	八
nine	kyu	九
ten	ju	十

Who do you think is tori and who is uke?

29

Glossary

adaptability
(uh-dapt-uh-BIH-lih-tee)
Ability to change to fit a new
or specific use or situation.

combat (KOM-bat)
Active fighting in a war.

contract (KON-trakt)
A legally binding agreement
between two or more parties.

counterclockwise
(kown-ter-KLOK-wyz)
Moving in the opposite
direction that the hands
of a clock move.

dojo (DOH-joh)
A training center for the
martial arts.

etiquette (EH-tih-kit)
The rules governing the
proper way to behave.

flexible (FLEK-sih-bul)
Capable of being bent.

forearm (FOR-arm)
The part of the human
arm between the elbow
and the wrist.

judogi (JOO-doh-gee)
A lightweight garment worn for martial arts, usually white loose-fitting pants and a white jacket.

kanji (KAHN-jee)
A Japanese system of writing based on borrowed or modified Chinese characters.

ligaments (LIH-guh-ments)
Tough bands of tissue that hold bones together.

samurai (SA-muh-ry)
A warrior serving a Japanese feudal lord and practicing a code of conduct which valued honor over life.

stance (STANS)
A way of standing.

submission (sub-MIH-shun)
An act of submitting to the authority or control of another.

Websites

Due to the changing nature of Internet links, PowerKids Press has developed an online list of websites related to the subject of this book. This site is updated regularly. Please use this link to access the list:
www.powerkidslinks.com/akgma/jujit/

Read More

Crean, Susan. *Discover Japan*. Discover Countries. New York: PowerKids Press, 2012.

O'Shei, Tim. *Jujitsu*. Blazers: Martial Arts. Mankato, MN: Capstone Press, 2009.

Robertson, Lauren. *The Best Book of Martial Arts*. New York: Kingfisher, 2003.

Index